THE LITTLE BOOK OF

RUM

TIPS

Andrew Langley

THE LITTLE BOOK OF

RUM

TIPS

BLOOMSBURY ABSOLUTE

LONDON · OXFORD · NEW YORK · NEW DELHI · SYDNEY

'There's naught, no doubt,
so much the spirit calms as rum
and true religion.'

George Gordon, Lord Byron
(1788–1824)

1. **Rum** is one of the world's great all-round drinks. It **is famed as a brilliant mixer in cocktails**, with anything from cola and tropical fruit to gin and eggs. **And it adds exotic drama to a host of dishes** such as ice cream, fruit cakes or even barbecued spare ribs. **But there's a lot more to rum than that.**

"Rum is famed as a brilliant mixer in cocktails and it adds exotic drama to a host of dishes. But there's a lot more to rum than that."

2. Like a fine brandy, **high-class rum deserves to be sipped – and savoured – on its own**. Pour a little into a proper spirit glass (a 'snifter') with a narrow top and a slightly rounded bowl. This traps and focuses the aromas for your nose to enjoy. Add nothing else to the glass.

"High-class rum deserves to be sipped – and savoured – on its own.

3. **Serve a good rum at room temperature to gain the most flavour.** If necessary, warm the glass in your hands a little and swill the liquid very gingerly round the bowl. This will mix oxygen with the rum and release the volatile oils which carry its wonderful tastes and aromas.

"Serve a good rum at room temperature to gain the most flavour."

4. **The first thrill is the smell. But take it gently.** As you raise the glass, you'll get the primary hints of the powerful fragrances coming from within. Then sniff cautiously with your mouth open – the powerful alcohol fumes rising up with the aroma can give your nose a big jolt.

"The first thrill is the smell.
But take it gently."

5. Next comes the first sip. **Keep the rum in your mouth for a moment, so it coats the whole of your tongue. Then swallow and breathe out.** Depending on the quality of the rum, you will get a large variety of flavours and tones, including maybe vanilla, honey and bitter chocolate. Think up your own description.

"Keep the rum in your mouth for a moment, so it coats the whole of your tongue. Then swallow and breathe out."

6. **Why do rums come in different colours?** This is partly to do with ageing in oak casks, which give colour and complexity to the spirit. Typically a white rum is aged for fewer than 3 years, a gold rum for up to 5 years and a dark rum for more than 6 years. Some dark rums also have caramel added.

" Why do rums come in different colours? "

7. **What are the different rums used for?** White rums are lighter and softer in taste, thus perfect for popular cocktails like Mojitos and Daiquiris. Gold rums are medium-bodied and are drunk on the rocks or in heftier cocktails. Dark rums tend to have the most robust flavours and are often sipped neat.

"What are the different rums used for?"

8. **Essential rum cocktail #1: the Mojito.** In a tall glass put 2 teaspoons of sugar, a few torn mint leaves and a splash of soda. Stir to dissolve the sugar. Add the freshly squeezed juice of 1 lime, a shot of good white rum and ice cubes. Top up with soda and a slice of lime.

"**Essential rum cocktail #1:** the Mojito."

9. **Glut of strawberries? Preserve them in rum!** Hull any undamaged strawberries and pop into a large stoneware jar called a *rumtopf*. Sprinkle with sugar and cover with good rum. Keep on adding cherries, raspberries and other fruit in the same way throughout the year. Serve at Christmas.

"Glut of strawberries?
Preserve them in rum!"

10.

Spiced rum is the Marmite of the drinks world. Many believe the added punch of cloves, cinnamon and other spices overwhelm rum's true charms. But **there are many spiced rums which are both zingy and subtle**, using local ingredients. Try Sailor Jerry or Chairman's Reserve.

"There are many spiced rums which are both zingy and subtle.

11.

Which rum has the most powerful flavour? There's no definite answer, but the leading contenders tend to come from Jamaica. This may be because some yeasty froth from each fermentation is saved for the next batch, and the Jamaicans believe this produces a stronger and fuller taste.

"Which rum has the most powerful flavour?"

12.

Essential rum cocktail #2: the Cuba Libre. Another lime-based old stager, but for a twist, add bitters to provide a bite. Fill a tall glass with ice, add a dash of Angostura Bitters (if using), the juice of 1 lime and a measure of gold rum. Top up with cola and garnish with a wedge of lime.

"Essential rum cocktail #2: the Cuba Libre."

13. **Find your inner Long John Silver with a tumbler of grog.** This is how pirates and British sailors traditionally took their rum. You'll need Pusser's Navy Rum (good and strong). Pop a cinnamon stick in a glass, add the rum, hot water, a sprinkle of brown sugar and fresh lime juice.

"Find your inner Long John Silver with a tumbler of grog."

14.

What is *cachaça*? **The basic ingredient for most rum is molasses,** a by-product of sugar production. **But some special rums are made with fresh sugar cane juice.** Brazil produces its own version of this, called *cachaça* – a light, fruity spirit which is becoming very hip.

"The basic ingredient for most rum is molasses, but some special rums are made with fresh sugar cane juice."

15. **Rum and pork are ideal partners.** Marinade a tenderloin of pork in a shot of dark rum, the same of soy sauce and 1 tablespoon each of chopped ginger and brown sugar, plus 4 tablespoons of olive oil for 2 hours. While you grill the meat, bring the excess marinade to a boil for a few seconds. Cool slightly and pour over the tenderloin.

"Rum and pork are ideal partners."

16. **Essential rum cocktail #3: the Planter's Punch.** The origins of this particular cocktail are murky, but it's a classic rum punch. In a shaker, shake up a shot of dark rum, the juice of 1 orange plus the same amount of pineapple juice, the juice of 1 lemon and 1 teaspoon each of grenadine and sugar syrup. Strain over ice and dash with Angostura Bitters.

"Essential rum cocktail #3:
the Planter's Punch."

17.

Which rums are best to use in cooking meat dishes? The answer is: all of them. But use your judgement. As a general rule, **the heftier flavours of dark rums go best with red meats, while white rums are suited to poultry and shellfish**.

"The heftier flavours of dark rums go best with red meats, while white rums are suited to poultry and shellfish."

18. **Here's a super-simple and speedy rum and chicken recipe.** Brown chicken thighs with butter and sage leaves. Add chicken stock to come halfway up the chicken, simmer for 5 minutes then add a double shot of light rum. Turn down low and cook for another 20 minutes.

"Here's a super-simple and speedy rum and chicken recipe...

19.

Rum and shallot sauce lights up any pepper steak. Once you've sautéed and removed the steak from the pan, pour off the excess fat. Soften chopped shallots in butter and deglaze with a little stock. Pour in a slug of dark rum and reduce quickly. Melt in more butter and anoint the rested steak.

"Rum and shallot sauce lights up any pepper steak."

20.

Rum and seafood is a match made in heaven, so **why not glaze your grilled prawns with rum**? Whisk together the juice and zest of 1 lime, 1 tablespoon of honey, grated ginger root, chopped garlic, a hint of cayenne and a shot of light rum. Boil and leave to cool. Pour over the prawns and refrigerate for 2 hours. Grill or skewer and barbecue.

"Why not glaze your grilled prawns with rum?"

21.

It's a classic combination, **but orange and rum make a velvety sauce for seared scallops**. Sear and remove the scallops from the pan, pour in a double shot of gold rum and scrape up any residue in the pan. Add the juice of 1 orange. Reduce for 1 minute then stir in a big knob of butter. Return the scallops to the pan and sprinkle with chopped parsley.

"Orange and rum make a velvety sauce for seared scallops."

22.

Essential rum cocktail #4: the Piña Colada. For a unique take on this classic, make this legendary blend of two rums with coconut. In a shaker, mix crushed ice, shots of dark and light rum and the same of pineapple juice, plus 30g of creamed coconut. Shake together, adding sugar syrup and lime juice to taste. Top with a cherry.

"Essential rum cocktail #4:
the Piña Colada.

23. **What's the secret of a great Dark 'n' Stormy?** Well, great dark rum full of flavour, for a start, and a good quality ginger beer (Fever Tree or similar). Some people add a little ginger cordial, others like a wedge of lime. Everyone likes a lot of ice.

"What's the secret of a great Dark 'n' Stormy?"

24.

Rum, quinoa and pepper: a veggie dream! Sauté chopped onion and garlic in oil. Stir in 1 can of black beans, oregano, ground cumin, coriander and chilli. Mix with 100g of cooked quinoa and the same of raisins plumped in rum. Stuff it all into roasted and skinned green peppers and bake for 20 minutes.

"Rum, quinoa and pepper: a veggie dream!

25.

For a truly Jamaican take on beef stew, brown beef chunks in oil, adding chopped onion and carrots, then minced green chilli and garlic. Pour in 60ml of dark rum and boil. Stir in beef stock to cover, plus bay leaves, allspice, 1 can of tomatoes and hot pepper sauce. Cook on a low heat for 90 minutes.

> **For a truly Jamaican take on beef stew...**

26. Rum fresh from ageing in a cask is very strong – between 60 and 70% by volume, if not higher. Most is cut (diluted) with water when it's bottled, going down to 45 to 55%. But **you can buy the liquor uncut – it is known as 'overproof rum' and it packs an amazing punch**.

"You can buy the liquor uncut – it is known as 'overproof rum' and it packs an amazing punch."

27. **The Zombie**, the infamous rum cocktail, **gets its name from the effects of its astounding alcohol level**. Shake together equal parts white rum, gold rum, dark rum, apricot brandy, pineapple juice and papaya juice, plus ice. Strain into a glass and add a shot of overproof rum. Go easy!

"The Zombie gets its name from the effects of its astounding alcohol level."

28.

Essential rum cocktail #5: the Daiquiri. This is the simplest of the classics. Put a shot of white rum into a cocktail shaker, along with the juice of half a lime, 1 teaspoon of sugar syrup and some ice. Shake well and strain into a well-chilled glass.

“Essential rum cocktail #5: the Daiquiri.”

29. **Cumberland Rum Nicky is a traditional Lake District treat.** Line a buttered pie dish with shortcrust pastry. Cover with 2 parts chopped dates and 1 part preserved ginger. Pour over a mix of melted butter, a little sugar and a shot of dark rum. Lattice with pastry strips and bake for 35 minutes.

"Cumberland Rum Nicky is a traditional Lake District treat.

30.

Crazy rum drink? Medicine? Aphrodisiac? Mamajuana lays claim to be all three. Loved in the Dominican Republic, it's an infusion of dark rum, red wine, honey and a mix of bark, spices and herbs. You can even buy the flavourings dried and packaged and make your own Mamajuana.

"Crazy rum drink? Medicine? Aphrodisiac? Mamajuana lays claim to be all three."

31.

Spiced rum stars in the Cable Car cocktail. First make a lemon sour – 2 tablespoons of lemon juice mixed with 1 tablespoon of sugar syrup. **In a shaker, combine** 2 parts **dark spiced rum**, 2 parts **lemon sour and** 1 part orange **curaçao**. Shake and strain into a glass decorated with orange zest.

"Spiced rum stars in the Cable Car cocktail. In a shaker, combine dark spiced rum, lemon sour and curaçao."

32. **Rum is a natural with pineapple.**
Peel and roll a whole pineapple
in sugar, chilli flakes and cracked
pepper. Dot with butter and roast in
a medium-hot oven for 30 minutes.
Meanwhile, whip up a can of
coconut cream with a shot of white
rum and then dollop this on the hot
pineapple slices.

"Rum is a natural with pineapple.

33.

The best ice cream? Rum and raisin!
Soak 150g of raisins in 225ml of dark
rum overnight. Whisk up 6 egg yolks
with 175g of sugar and 500ml of
milk. Warm gently until it thickens.
Combine with the drained raisins,
2 tablespoons of rum, a dash of
vanilla essence and 500ml of cream.
Churn and freeze.

"The best ice cream? Rum and raisin!

34.

Essential rum cocktail #6: the Hurricane. It's luridly red – unlike a real hurricane – but very moreish. Fill a shaker with shots of light and dark rum, plus 1 tablespoon each of grenadine, lime juice and passion fruit syrup, and a little sugar syrup to taste. Shake and strain into a glass over ice.

"Essential rum cocktail #6: the Hurricane.

35. **For legendary Bananas Foster –** weirdly named after the 1950s boss of the New Orleans Crime Commission – **melt together** 60g of **butter**, 125g of **dark sugar and** a pinch of **cinnamon**. **Stir in** a shot of **banana liqueur, add** 4 **bananas and fry** until very soft. **Flambé** the lot **in a shot of gold rum**.

"For legendary Bananas Foster, melt together butter, dark sugar and cinnamon. Stir in banana liqueur, add bananas and fry. Flambé in a shot of gold rum.

36.

A must for Christmas pud – and a lot more – **here's the traditional Cumbrian recipe for a delicious rum butter**. Very gently melt 225g of butter and mix in 225g of dark brown sugar. Away from the heat, stir in a wine glass of dark rum and half a grated nutmeg. Pour into a sterilised jar and seal.

"**Here's the traditional Cumbrian recipe for a delicious rum butter...**"

37. **The buttered rum is a seafarers' classic.** Whisk 25g of melted butter with 1 tablespoon of maple syrup and a shot of dark rum. Add orange peel studded with 3 cloves, then 50ml of boiling water. Decant into a mug and slot in a cinnamon stick.

"The buttered rum is a seafarers' classic.

38.

The Mai Tai cocktail is otherwise known as 'Trader Vic's', after its inventor. It **calls for the finest dark Jamaican rum** (8 parts) and **orgeat**, an almond syrup (1 part). Shake these up with 3 parts **lime juice**, 2 parts **orange curaçao and** 1 part **sugar syrup**, plus ice.

"The Mai Tai cocktail calls for the finest dark Jamaican rum, orgeat, lime juice, orange curaçao and sugar syrup."

39.

New Englanders just love Joe Froggers, and **making these rum-flavoured cookies is super speedy**. Mix 380g of flour, 1 teaspoon of baking soda, ¼ teaspoon each of nutmeg, ginger, cloves and allspice. Add 75ml of hot water, 350ml of molasses, a slug of dark rum, 100g of butter and 225g of sugar. Chill for 1 hour then roll out the dough and cut into rounds. Bake in a hot oven for 10 minutes.

"Making these rum-flavoured cookies is super speedy..."

40. In Central Europe, they **keep out the winter cold with** *Jagertree*. In a saucepan, heat equal parts spiced rum, red wine, tea, schnapps and orange juice with a cinnamon stick, a few cloves and 2 lemon slices. Simmer for 5 minutes and pour into glasses, with sugar to taste.

"**Keep out the winter cold with *Jagertree*.**"

41. **For a quick, quirky dessert, pair rum with oranges.** Peel 8 oranges and cut into 1cm-thick slices. Spread on a dish, add a double shot of dark rum and the zest from 2 of the oranges. Make caramel by gently melting 225g of sugar in a saucepan, and pour over the fruit.

"For a quick, quirky, dessert, pair rum with oranges."

42. **Catalans make an explosive rum punch called *cremat*.** Gently warm 335ml of rum and 225ml of Spanish brandy. Pour into a flame-proof bowl with 2 cinnamon sticks, 3 tablespoons of sugar and lemon zest. Then light it (beware the flare!). When the flames die down, stir in 1 litre of strong black coffee.

"Catalans make an explosive rum punch called *cremat*."

43.

Weirdest cocktail name? It has to be Sandra Buys a Dog. We don't know who Sandra was, but the recipe is simple enough. Fill a tall glass with ice and dash in some bitters. Add a shot of dark rum, a shot of *anejo* (aged) rum, the same of orange juice and 75ml of cranberry juice.

"Weirdest cocktail name? It has to be Sandra Buys a Dog."

44.

Another quick, easy but impressive rum dessert. **Halve a pink grapefruit** and **cut round the segments** to loosen them. **Brush with dark rum, sprinkle with brown sugar, ground cinnamon and** a pinch of **cayenne pepper and pop under a hot grill** for about 5 minutes.

"Halve a pink grapefruit, cut round the segments, brush with dark rum, sprinkle with brown sugar, ground cinnamon and cayenne pepper and pop under a hot grill."

45.

Custard gains a lot from a shot of rum. Heat 150ml each of milk and cream with a splash of vanilla essence. Separately whisk 3 egg yolks, 3 tablespoons of sugar and 1 tablespoon of cornflour, then slowly fold in the creamy mixture. Heat again and stir in a measure of dark rum.

"Custard gains a lot from a shot of rum.

46.

Rum for breakfast? **For the best breakfast ever, whip together** a slug of **light rum**, 3 **eggs**, 2 tablespoons of **sugar**, a little **vanilla essence**, 1 teaspoon each of **cinnamon** and **nutmeg and** a pinch of **salt. Soak slices of sweet bread** (such as challah or brioche) **in the mixture and fry** in a grill pan with butter and serve with maple syrup.

"For the best breakfast ever, whip together light rum, eggs, sugar, vanilla essence, cinnamon, nutmeg and salt. Soak slices of sweet bread in the mixture and fry."

47. **Home-made fruit infusions are a good way of transforming cheap rum.** White rums go well with mango, passion fruit or limes. The heftier tones of dark rum work wonders with bananas, pineapple or coconut. Chop the bigger fruits and mix 1 part fruit to 1 part rum. Drink after 3 days.

"Home-made fruit infusions are a good way of transforming cheap rum.

48. Here are **three unusual cane-sugar rums to look out for**. The best *rhum agricole* comes from the French-speaking island of Martinique. The Haitians make *clairin*, the only completely chemical-free rum in the world, and Mexico produces a raw light-brown rum called *charanda*.

"Three unusual cane-sugar rums to look out for..."

49. Once it's been opened, **a bottle of rum should be drunk or otherwise used up within 6 months**. After the cap seal is broken, alcohol gradually evaporates and oxygen from outside mingles with the rum inside. This can alter the flavour, the colour and the strength.

"A bottle of rum should be drunk or otherwise used up within 6 months."

50. In theory, a bottle of rum will last forever – as long as it's unopened. Even so, **it's best to store your rum in a cool place where the temperature stays much the same**. Keep it away from direct sunlight, which can not only heat but cause colour and chemical changes to the contents.

"It's best to store your rum in a cool place where the temperature stays much the same."

Andrew Langley

Andrew Langley is **a knowledgeable food and drink writer.** Among his formative influences he lists a season picking grapes in Bordeaux, several years of raising sheep and chickens in Wiltshire and two decades drinking his grandmother's tea. He has written books on a number of Scottish and Irish whisky distilleries and is the editor of the highly regarded anthology of the writings of the legendary Victorian chef Alexis Soyer.

"A knowledgeable food and drink writer."

Little Books of Tips from
Bloomsbury Absolute

Aga	Gin
Allotment	Golf
Avocado	Herbs
Beer	Prosecco
Cake Decorating	Rum
Cheese	Spice
Cider	Tea
Coffee	Vodka
Fishing	Whisky
Gardening	Wine

If you enjoyed this book, try...

THE LITTLE BOOK OF

VODKA

TIPS

"For the 007 experience, put crushed ice, a shot of vodka and French vermouth in a shaker and shake well."

"A Bloody Mary gives you (almost all) your five a day in one cocktail."

BLOOMSBURY ABSOLUTE
Bloomsbury Publishing Plc
50 Bedford Square, London, WC1B 3DP, UK

BLOOMSBURY, BLOOMSBURY ABSOLUTE, the Diana logo and the Absolute Press
logo are trademarks of Bloomsbury Publishing Plc

A catalogue record for this book is available from the British Library.
Library of Congress Cataloguing-in-Publication data has been applied for.

ISBN: 9781472973313
2 4 6 8 10 9 7 5 3 1

Printed and bound in China by Toppan Leefung Printing

Bloomsbury Publishing Plc makes every effort to ensure that the papers used in the
manufacture of our books are natural, recyclable products made from wood grown in
well-managed forests. Our manufacturing processes conform to the environmental
regulations of the country of origin.
    To find out more about our authors and books visit www.bloomsbury.com and sign
up for our newsletters.

> **For the 007 experience, put crushed ice, a shot of vodka and French vermouth in a shaker and shake well.**

> **A Bloody Mary gives you (almost all) your five a day in one cocktail.**

BLOOMSBURY ABSOLUTE
Bloomsbury Publishing Plc
50 Bedford Square, London, WC1B 3DP, UK

BLOOMSBURY, BLOOMSBURY ABSOLUTE, the Diana logo and the Absolute Press
logo are trademarks of Bloomsbury Publishing Plc

First published in Great Britain 2019
Copyright © Andrew Langley, 2019
Cover image © Getty Images

A catalogue record for this book is available from the British Library.
Library of Congress Cataloguing-in-Publication data has been applied for.

ISBN: 9781472973313
2 4 6 8 10 9 7 5 3 1

Printed and bound in China by Toppan Leefung Printing

Bloomsbury Publishing Plc makes every effort to ensure that the papers used in the
manufacture of our books are natural, recyclable products made from wood grown in
well-managed forests. Our manufacturing processes conform to the environmental
regulations of the country of origin.

To find out more about our authors and books visit www.bloomsbury.com and sign
up for our newsletters.